the

everyman

being God's man...

by pursuing friendships

series

Real Men. Real Life. Powerful Truth.

Stephen Arterburn

Kenny Luck & Todd Wendorff

WATERBROOK
PRESS

BEING GOD'S MAN...BY PURSUING FRIENDSHIPS
PUBLISHED BY WATERBROOK PRESS
2375 Telstar Drive, Suite 160
Colorado Springs, Colorado 80920
A division of Random House, Inc.

All Scripture quotations, unless otherwise indicated, are taken from the *Holy Bible, New International Version®*. NIV®. Copyright © 1973, 1978, 1984 by International Bible Society. Used by permission of Zondervan Publishing House. All rights reserved. Scripture quotations marked (MSG) are taken from *The Message*. Copyright © by Eugene H. Peterson 1993, 1994, 1995. Used by permission of NavPress Publishing Group. Scripture quotations marked (NASB) are taken from the *New American Standard Bible®* (NASB). © Copyright The Lockman Foundation 1960, 1962, 1963, 1968, 1971, 1972, 1973, 1975, 1977, 1995. Used by permission. (www.Lockman.org). Scripture quotations marked (NLT) are taken from the *Holy Bible, New Living Translation,* copyright © 1996. Used by permission of Tyndale House Publishers, Inc., Wheaton, Illinois 60189. All rights reserved.

ISBN 1-57856-684-3

Published in association with the literary agency of Alive Communications, Inc., 7680 Goddard Street, Suite 200, Colorado Springs, CO 80920.

Printed in the United States of America
2003—First Edition

10 9 8 7 6 5 4 3 2 1

contents

welcome to the every man
Bible study series

As Christian men, we crave true-to-life, honest, and revealing Bible study curricula that will equip us for the battles that rage in our lives. We are looking for resources that will get us into our Bibles in the context of mutually accountable relationships with other men. But like superheroes who wear masks and work hard to conceal their true identities, most of us find ourselves isolated and working alone on the major issues we face. Many of us present a carefully designed public self, while hiding our private self from view. This is not God's plan for us.

Let's face it. We all have trouble being honest with ourselves, particularly in front of other men.

As developers of a men's ministry, we believe that many of the problems among Christian men today are direct consequences of an inability to practice biblical openness—being honest about our struggles, questions, and temptations—and to connect with one another. Our external lives may be in order, but storms of unprocessed conflict, loss, and fear are eroding our resolve to maintain integrity. Sadly, hurting Christian men are flocking to unhealthy avenues of relief instead of turning to God's Word and to one another.

We believe the solution to this problem lies in creating opportunities for meaningful relationships among men. That's why we designed this Bible study series to be thoroughly interactive. When a man practices biblical openness with other men, he moves from secrecy to candor, from isolation to connection, and from pretense to authenticity.

Kenny and Todd developed the study sessions at Saddleback Church in Lake Forest, California, where they teach the men's morning Bible studies. There, men hear an outline of the Bible passage, read the verses together, and then answer a group discussion question at their small-group tables. The teaching pastor then facilitates further discussion within the larger group.

This approach is a huge success for many reasons, but the key is that, deep down, men really do want close friendships with other guys. We don't enjoy living on the barren islands of our own secret struggles. However, many men choose to process life, relationships, and pressures individually because they fear the vulnerability required in small-group gatherings. *Suppose someone sees behind my carefully constructed image? Suppose I encounter rejection after revealing one of my worst sins?* Men willingly take risks in business and the stock market, sports and recreation, but we do not easily risk our inner lives.

Many church ministries are now helping men win this battle, providing them with opportunities to experience Christian male companionship centered in God's Word. This study series aims to supplement and expand that good work around the country. If these lessons successfully reach you, then they will also reach every relationship and domain that you influence. That is our heartfelt prayer for every man in your group.

how to use this study guide

As you prepare for each session, first review the **Key Verse** and **Goals for Growth,** which reveal the focus of the study at hand. Discuss as a group whether or not you will commit to memorizing the Key Verse for each session. The **Head Start** section then explains why these goals are necessary and worthwhile. Each member of your small group should complete the **Connect with the Word** section *before* the small-group sessions. Consider this section to be your personal Bible study for the week. This will ensure that everyone has spent some time interacting with the biblical texts for that session and is prepared to share responses and personal applications. (You may want to mark or highlight any questions that were difficult or particularly meaningful, so you can focus on those during the group discussion.)

When you gather in your small group, you'll begin by reading aloud the **Head Start** section to remind everyone of the focus for the current session. The leader will then invite the group to share any questions, concerns, insights, or comments arising from their personal Bible study during the past week. If your group is large, consider breaking into subgroups of three or four people (no more than six) at this time.

Next get into **Connect with the Group,** starting with the **Group Opener.** These openers are designed to get at the heart of each week's lesson. They focus on how the men in your group relate to the passage and topic you are about to discuss. The group leader will read the opener for that week's session aloud and then facilitate interaction on the **Discussion Questions** that follow. (Remember: Not everyone has to offer an answer for every question.)

Leave time after your discussion to complete the **Standing Strong** exercises, which challenge each man to consider, *What's my next move?* As you openly express your thoughts to the group, you'll be able to hold one another accountable to reach for your goals.

Finally, close in **prayer,** either in your subgroups or in the larger group. You may want to use this time to reflect on and respond to what God has done in your group during the session. Also invite group members to share their personal joys and concerns, and use this as "grist" for your prayer time together.

By way of review, each lesson is divided into the following sections:

To be read or completed *before* the small-group session:
- **Key Verse**
- **Goals for Growth**
- **Head Start**
- **Connect with the Word** (home Bible study: 30-40 minutes)

To be completed *during* the small-group session:
- Read aloud the **Head Start** section (5 minutes)
- Discuss personal reaction to **Connect with the Word** (10 minutes)
- **Connect with the Group** (includes the **Group Opener** and discussion of the heart of the lesson: 30-40 minutes)
- **Standing Strong** (includes having one person pray for the group; challenges each man to take action: 20 minutes)

spiritual castaways

Remember the movie *Cast Away,* starring Tom Hanks? It's a modern-day *Gilligan's Island,* but with no Skipper, Mary Ann, Ginger, Professor, Gilligan, or the Howells. It's not funny to watch, either; it's painful. Hanks plays Chuck Noland, who's riding in a FedEx cargo plane when it drifts off course somewhere over the Pacific Ocean and loses its communications in the middle of a typhoon. Before the crew can reestablish radio contact, the plane crashes into the ocean. Miraculously, Chuck survives and washes ashore on his own lonely little island. So begins his long and painful odyssey as a castaway.

Fast-forward to his miraculous rescue four years later...

Chuck's old girlfriend reminisces with him about the rescue efforts at the time of his disappearance. She spreads out the old search grid on the kitchen table and shows Chuck where the effort had focused, based on the original flight plan. Then she slides her finger hundreds of miles across the map over to where he was actually rescued. The inability of the pilot to report his position, combined with a slow drift off course, sealed Chuck's fate and doomed the rescue before it even began.

Now, we're only talking about a Hollywood movie, but just as severed communication doomed Chuck to being a lonely castaway, we've seen firsthand how the lack of communication and connection among men has created a whole culture of spiritual castaways. Pulled off course in their walks with God, not reporting their personal or spiritual status to anyone, men become isolated. No one really knows them or where they are in their private struggles. Their spiritual compasses are definitely off track. Time passes, and when the typhoons of temptation strike, they drift *way* off course. Unfortunately, many men do not even have the chance to get rescued because they were never checking in with anyone.

Here's what's working against us: We are traveling through life unconnected and unexamined, carefully projecting an image that says, "I'm okay." But privately, deep down, we battle huge inner turmoil and conflict that stem from life's normal pressures and are exacerbated by our character flaws.

Those emotions have to be expressed somehow; we don't live in a vacuum. The world, the flesh, and Satan exploit our isolation. Some of us who feel unconnected choose avenues of relief and comfort outside of God's plan, which bring harm to our relationship with Him and with others. At every men's conference we lead, we encounter men who fess up to using Internet porn, having illicit affairs, and ingesting way too many substances their bodies were not designed to handle. Others immerse themselves in their work, a sports team, or some hobby to help them deal with the stresses of life. Unfortunately, these diversions are exactly that—diversions. They don't make us better men. We have found that men who are not progressing personally, spiritually, or relationally are in those ruts because they will not risk connecting with another man.

But we need to connect. We were designed to connect.

Men do not become men in the company of women. We become men in the company of other men. As you will see in the lessons ahead, this is the way God wants His men to go. Pursuing healthy friendship is a way of life that provides help when we need it most. Wherever you find men watching one another's backs, grabbing each other (you know what I mean), and caring enough to confront in order to help a friend become God's man, you find men who are growing their characters and spiritual lives, men who no longer live as spiritual castaways.

As you proceed through this Bible study, determine to hold up a mirror to your life and ask yourself some tough questions. Spend plenty of time in personal reflection and honest dialogue with God and, optimally, with other men. Whether you are doing this study individually or in a group, realize that honesty with yourself, with God, and with others will produce the greatest results.

Our prayer is that you will be moved to embrace God's plan for friendship and will experience His promised blessings as you risk going deeper in your relationships with other men.

the myth of isolation

Key Verse

Though one may be overpowered, two can defend themselves. A cord of three strands is not quickly broken. (Ecclesiastes 4:12)

Goals for Growth

- Understand the danger of isolation.
- Recognize that isolation stunts spiritual growth and opens us up to spiritual attack.
- Commit to ending relational or emotional isolation.

Head Start

The number one dilemma facing God's men today is isolation. More than at any other time in history, men feel emotionally and relationally cut off from other men. If it weren't so, they wouldn't be spending billions of dollars on sexually explicit Internet sites to find relief from their loneliness. Sure, we have friends and we certainly lead busy lives, but as a general condition, we males are not connected to one another for any deep purposes (although we hope your group is an exception).

When a guy is under pressure or his relationships are suffering or life has simply thrown him one too many curves, he tends to keep his suffering to himself. This isn't healthy for any man, and it's a definite no-no for God's man. You see, there's more to isolation than just not having someone to talk to. Isolation weakens our defenses. We are engaged in a spiritual battle every day, and one side or the other is winning at each moment. So the question is, Who will prevail in the various domains of your life today—the dark forces aligned with the world and the devil, or God and His kingdom? In his book *Things Only Men Know,* Preston Gillham put it this way, "The Enemy of God and man perpetuates a uniquely masculine attack—isolation."

Overcoming isolation, then, is not about getting and giving warm fuzzies or an occasional high-five. It involves a war for your spiritual well-being, your effectiveness for God, and your impact on those closest to you. What God's man needs to clearly understand is that isolation from other men is not just bad, it's *deadly.*

Connect with the Word

Read Ecclesiastes 4:9-12.

1. What is being compared and contrasted in this passage?

2. What are the downsides of isolation? What are the upsides of supportive friendships?

3. When is the condition of isolation most clearly seen and felt?

4. When an isolated man falls down, what happens?

5. Why do you think Solomon used the word *pity* to describe an isolated man who has fallen? What obvious outcomes illicit sorrow for that man?

Read 1 Peter 5:8.

6. Why is Satan compared to a lion? What does this imply about his approach or methods of attack?

7. What is the devil's constant preoccupation?

8. What factors give a lion the best chance for catching and killing its prey? What factors make it more difficult?

9. What condition automatically makes a man a prospective meal for the devil? When are you most liable to becoming a tasty nugget yourself?

Connect with the Group

Group Opener
Read the group opener aloud and discuss the questions that follow.
(Suggestion: As you begin your group discussion time in each of the fol-
lowing sessions, consider forming smaller groups of three to six men. This
will allow more time for discussion and give everyone an opportunity to
share their thoughts and struggles.)

When my wife, Chrissy, asked me to rally the men of our couples
group to help move a family, I [Kenny] reluctantly agreed (because I
hate to help move). Who enjoys lugging heavy refrigerators and tons
of boxes, especially when it's somebody else's junk? But Chrissy had
become acquainted with Tina (the wife) at church, and she saw an
opportunity for us to meet a need. Tina's husband, Hans, was certainly grateful when so many helping hands showed up that Saturday
morning. We moved everything, including their redwood Jacuzzi, to
their new address just a mile away. While moving is not my first
choice for male bonding (I'll take a half-day mountain-bike trip any
day), there's something about carrying furniture and lifting boxes
that bonds people. And the pepperoni pizza party afterward never
hurts either. Despite my bad attitude regarding the move, by the
end of the day I felt that we were beginning the start of a special
friendship.

The next time I ran into Hans was a month later at church.
I asked him how the move finished up and then mentioned how
I thought God used the time to bring us together that day. When I
said that, his eyes immediately filled with tears.

"Hans, are you okay?"

"I was so alone," he choked out.

"What did you say?" I didn't think I had heard him correctly.

He took a deep breath and said again, very clearly, "Kenny, I was so alone."

In that moment, Hans defined what I believe is the number one dilemma facing Christian men: isolation.[1]

Discussion Questions

a. Describe a time, if any, when you have felt like Hans did? What is the primary way you cope during times of isolation and loneliness?

---

1. Stephen Arterburn and Kenny Luck, *Every Man, God's Man* (Colorado Springs: WaterBrook Press, 2003), 141.

b. Do you have friends in your life right now who know about your true state of life? about your times of loneliness? about the times you fall down or sin? What can you do to deepen these friendships? If you don't have friends like this, what steps can you take to begin developing close friendships with other men?

c. When, if ever, has your isolation negatively impacted your spiritual life? your relationships? your marriage?

d. In what area(s) of your life are you being overpowered by the roaring lion? Have you opened up to another man about it? If not, why?

e. In what way, if any, does isolation (or keeping that area "under the radar") play a role in your vulnerability to spiritual attack?

f. Why do you think men continue living isolated and defeated spiritual lives? What lies do you think Satan tells a man to keep him isolated and open to attack?

g. What can we do as a group to protect one another from becoming isolated?

Standing Strong

What one thing, more than any other, has this week's study motivated you to do? What specific steps will you take?

Write a one-sentence prayer expressing to God your desire to overcome isolation and connect more deeply with other men:

Be prepared to share your progress with the group at your next meeting.

the command to connect

Key Verse

Pursue righteousness, faith, love and peace, along with those who call on the Lord out of a pure heart. (2 Timothy 2:22)

Goals for Growth

- Realize that connecting with other men is not optional.
- Understand that connecting with other men is of practical importance to your spiritual growth.
- Commit to pursuing and deepening male friendships.

Head Start

The apostle Paul wrote to Corinthian men, "The eye can never say to the hand, 'I don't need you.' The head can't say to the feet, 'I don't need you'" (1 Corinthians 12:21, NLT). His point was clear: Stop acting as if you don't need one another. What he knew, and what we see, is that when men are "doing life" with other men who share their commitment to spiritual growth, they can sustain their momentum and achieve personal changes faster than if they attempt to go it alone. No big mystery; that's God's plan.

When we ask guys if they are connected spiritually somewhere, they often reply that they are in a couples' Bible study. Then we ask them if, in their couples' group, they have ever talked about their struggles with porn on the Internet or with hot babes at work. We haven't heard a positive response yet.

The fact is, when we're in the company of women—including our wives—we simply don't discuss the things we need to deal with as men. And lust and temptation aren't the only topics we need to talk about. We need to connect with men in significant communication regarding every domain of life, dealing candidly with the specific dynamics unique to men in marriage, career, and parenting. Most important, we need to be real with one another about our progress in commitment to Jesus Christ as He seeks to influence each of those areas. What we said in the introduction bears repeating: Men become men in the company of other men. Ask any warrior in any culture. And for God's man, who wants to do life God's way, connecting with other men is not optional.

Connect with the Word

Read 2 Timothy 2:20-22.

1. What's the central message of verse 20?

2. What actions does Paul encourage God's man to take in verse 22? Is this cowardly? Why or why not?

3. According to verse 22, what will play a critical role for God's man in reaching his spiritual goals? Why do you think Timothy's friend and mentor, Paul, stressed this?

4. How does the Bible describe the men Timothy needs to run with?

5. In practical terms, what does it mean to "pursue righteousness" with other men?

6. What does the passage imply about how we should fight temptation?

Read Hebrews 3:13; 10:23-25.

7. What specific encouragements are mentioned in these verses? How are they connected?

8. What are the goals of friendship according to these verses?

9. What are God's men mindful of as they encourage and sharpen one another in their faith (verse 25)? Why is that important?

10. How do these verses change your perspective on the *purpose* and
    importance of friendships?

Connect with the Group

Group Opener
Why do men generally act as if they don't need one another? Be sure
to talk about your own experience here!

Discussion Questions
a. What is your primary purpose in friendship? Does it line up
   with the purpose described in Hebrews 3:13 and 10:24?
   Explain.

b. What is your level of connection with other men right now? Explain. What specific struggles or frustrations have you experienced when you've tried to connect on a deeper level?

c. When, if ever, have you connected with another man on a deeper level? What do you think helped you connect at this level?

d. In 2 Timothy 2:22, Paul encouraged Timothy to connect with other godly men. In light of this passage, consider your three closest friendships and, on a scale of 1 to 10 (1 = poor; 10 = excellent), rate your level of connection in the areas of encouragement, honesty, and intimacy.

Friend: _____

    Encouragement:

    Honesty:

    Integrity:

Friend: _____

    Encouragement:

    Honesty:

    Integrity:

Friend: _____

    Encouragement:

    Honesty:

    Integrity:

Share your answers with the group and then discuss what specific actions you could take to develop close friendships or deepen your connection in existing ones?

Standing Strong

Based on what you discovered from this week's study, to what extent do you think you are spiritually connected with other men? Explain.

What risks are you willing to take to achieve a connection with other men that produces significant spiritual gains?

Write down a specific request you would like to see God answer regarding your friendships:

connecting to character

Key Verse

Become wise by walking with the wise; hang out with fools and watch your life fall to pieces. (Proverbs 13:20, MSG)

Goals for Growth

- Realize the importance of character in choosing our friends.
- Recognize the impact that others' character has on us.
- Commit to developing both godly character and godly relationships.

Head Start

We all remember the cliques in junior high and high school. Kids usually fell into one of several categories: jocks, nerds, the "in" crowd, the band, stoners, or honor students. Each clique had its own lingo, ways of thinking, and lists of activities or qualifications to officially belong.

Which clique did you identify with? How long was your hair—or what color was it?

The myth is that we will eventually grow out of a clique mentality, become more tolerant of different kinds of people, and become independent and mature. The reality is that cliques and their influences among men survive and thrive. As adults, we simply call cliques "our friends," but many of the dynamics are identical. We still gravitate toward people who act like us, look like us, like the things we like, and do what we do—for better or for worse. The one big difference between then and now is that much more is at stake, especially for God's man.

Like meat soaking in a marinade, we soak up the character of our close friends. As Proverbs 13:20 says, "He who walks with the wise grows wise, but a companion of fools suffers harm." Our friends rub off on us, both consciously and subconsciously, which leads to changes in our convictions and conduct. So the question is: *Who is rubbing off on you?*

Connect with the Word

Read Psalm 101.

1. What was David's primary goal in life? What are the specific character qualities David wanted for his life?

2. What character quality was he looking for in his associates? Why? What was at stake?

3. What warning signs tipped him off to the types of men he did not want to hang with?

4. What role did faithful men play in David's life (verse 6)?

5. At the end of the psalm, what was David's conclusion about who he would allow to influence him?

Connect with the Group

Group Opener

Read the group opener aloud and discuss the questions that follow.

Junior high was rough for me (Todd). I decided to rebel against authority and see what it was like. I had a very strong father who was

The Law in our home. I had just completed five years of private school and was sick of following the rules. So I began to experiment with drugs and alcohol. My friends didn't help much. They had uninvolved parents and ultimate freedom to do anything they wanted to. We'd wander the hill I grew up on and look for ways to be juvenile delinquents.

The final straw came on the evening when my father went to school and discovered the incredibly disrespectful attitude I'd developed toward my teachers. The next evening he called me into his den—an intimidating room where his safari animal trophies stared out at me from the walls. He had a three-decker organ in one corner of the room, and a couch, coffee table, and desk in the other. The minute I walked in, I knew I was toast.

All he had to say was, "Son, I've been to school, and I know what's going on." I fell into his arms and began to weep. As I wept, he told me one thing I will never forget: "Todd, there are two roads in life, and you are headed down the wrong one." He then told me to go to school the next day and change my friends. Cut it off at the root; eliminate the influence to change the behavior.

It worked. The next day, as a punk eighth grader, I abandoned my old friends and searched out a new crowd. My new friends were athletes and were heavily involved in school. Everything changed for me that year.

Discussion Questions

a. What were your junior-high years like? In what ways can you relate to my (Todd's) experience?

b. Which childhood friends were good for you? Which were bad influences? Why?

c. How would you describe your closest friends today? How do their priorities line up with your own? How do you know that a friend is influencing you negatively?

d. In what specific ways are your friends ministering to you these days?

e. Which particular character quality described in Psalm 101 inspires you personally? Why?

f. What specific indicators tell you that you need to break away from a friend or friends and find some new ones? What steps do you need to take to make that break?

g. What character qualities make you a positive influence on your friends? What about you is rubbing off on them?

h. Who, in this group, is rubbing off on you? Which of their qualities are you absorbing?

Standing Strong

Share with the group what you personally want to see come out of
your connection with them.

Pray for your friends, asking God to empower you to help them
become all that He made them to be. Also pray for an opportunity
to be used this week in the life of a friend, or if you have let an opportunity slip through the cracks, commit now to helping in a practical way.

the seriousness of support

Key Verse

A friend loves at all times, and a brother is born for adversity. (Proverbs 17:17)

Goals for Growth

- Realize that personal support is vital for men.
- Identify the kinds of support each man needs.
- Examine our willingness to be available to other men as a source of support.

Head Start

A men's small group is a great place for what we call the Four Cs: connection (mutuality), confession (authenticity), caring (ministry), and completion (maturity). We find that guys who meet frequently, who care about the spiritual welfare of their friends, and who can talk honestly about their struggles make steady progress personally, spiritually, and relationally. In a men's small group, secrets lose their power as God's people become God's presence and deliver God's provision for individuals in the group.

More specifically, God's plan is not for a man to turn to himself for answers when he is in crisis. Rather, he is called to turn to God and to His people for help and support. For men, turning to God alone seems fine, even preferred, because they can avoid the potential embarrassment that comes with vulnerability and confession. After all, we have our images to maintain and our egos to preserve!

Most men will, at great cost, choose isolation and endure frustration or unrelenting loneliness just to protect themselves. The great failing of this approach is that the longer a man remains unsupported and alone with his struggles, the worse they become.

On the other hand, men everywhere are discovering that they aren't alone in their struggles with their marriages, their finances, their spiritual growth, and their careers—other men share those same struggles. As King Solomon reflected, "There is nothing new under the sun" (Proverbs 1:9).

Connect with the Word

Read 2 Timothy 1:15-18; 2 Timothy 4:9-13.

1. According to these passages, what does it look like for one man to support another? What, specifically, does it look like in today's world?

2. What is being compared and contrasted in 1:15-18? What did Phygelus and Hermogenes do when the chips were down?

3. How does the passage describe Onesiphorus (which means "help bringer" in Greek)?

4. What was Paul's experience with Onesiphorus in the past? What do you think Paul's first thought was when he saw Onesiphorus in the confines of a prison?

5. What do we learn from Onesiphorus about helping other men?

6. How many men do you see in Paul's life in 4:9-13? What roles did they play?

Connect with the Group

Group Opener
Read the group opener aloud and discuss the questions that follow.

Jay's men's group meets every other Friday morning at a local coffee-house, and while it is hard to rally the troops at 6:30 A.M., no one complains. They've been meeting for the last three years and are now accustomed to stepping into the hard spaces of one another's lives. They are so connected that no subject is taboo, especially if one of them is struggling with something. These men conduct spiritual business, study God's Word for advice they can trust, share their weaknesses with one another, pray for one another, and hold one another accountable to live as God's men.

Recently, Shaun reported that he hasn't visited Internet porn sites as he used to do. Ed said that his business trip was uneventful and that he shared his faith with a guy on the plane. Matt described the "good flow" that he and his wife, Carol, have been enjoying, which was an answer to prayer after his previous week's doghouse tale. When Jeff announced that his sister was recently diagnosed with

Hodgkin's disease, Travis felt led to offer Jeff a frequent flyer ticket to Denver to see his ailing sister. As for Jay, he took advantage of the time to confess that he is struggling to reconnect with his wife, Alene, and asked for advice on how to break through feelings of resentment that kept him from loving his wife the way God loves him.

We've learned that guys who meet frequently care about the spiritual welfare of their brothers and can honestly talk about the struggles and challenges they face. In a men's small group, secrets lose their power as God's Word is brought to bear on the issues at hand. Besides, it feels good to have someone watching your back. That's how God's man feels connected.[2]

Discussion Questions

a. List some characteristics of Jay's group that are like and unlike your own men's group? In what ways could each group improve?

---

2.   Adapted from Arterburn and Luck, *Every Man, God's Man*, 145-6.

b. Based on this week's Scripture passages, what do God's men do for one another?

c. What does refreshing (breathing new life into, encouraging) a brother look like today in practical terms?

d. Onesiphorus stepped into Paul's life when things were darkest. What does this tell you about the kind of man he was? Why is it often hard for men to step into another man's problems or needs?

e. Why is it hard for men to receive help from another man? What is your experience with this?

f. What is the spiritual impact on a man when he receives support from others? Relate a personal story about this, if possible.

Standing Strong

In what area(s) of your life do you need the support of your brothers in Christ?

Who do you know that is going through a rough time these days? What can you do to support him in a tangible way and help him experience God's presence?

Name one of your three closest friends and make the following commitment:

I will call or get together with _____ for support in the following area:

the courage to confess

Key Verse

Make this your common practice: Confess your sins to each other and pray for each other so that you can live together whole and healed. (James 5:16, MSG)

Goals for Growth

- Recognize the need to practice biblical openness and confession with other men.
- Understand the consequences of living a secret life of sin.
- Embrace the practice of being honest with God, with ourselves, and with others.

Head Start

If you haven't figured this out by now, women spell intimacy T–A–L–K.

When emotions surface, women must verbally process them until no meat is left on the bone. Have you ever noticed that when a woman is feeling stressed out or angry, she will often call a friend to talk it over? Women are quick to express their feelings to others because they are hard-wired by God to be relational, nurturing, and emotionally connected. The bottom line is: These wonderfully complex creatures deal with their feelings.

We men, however, tend to run for the hills—all alone—when it comes to dealing with our emotions. We are not good at facing our feelings. Most of us have been trained to treat our emotions like smelly socks that we stash in the back of a drawer, as far away from us as possible.

When a man's emotions surface, the Sweeper (as we call him) comes in to methodically and logically neutralize the threat that a rogue emotion might present. He's that subconscious character in every man who works to eliminate emotions and makes logical arguments for acting the opposite way. His job is to keep any touchy situation from heating up too much, while sweeping any stray emotions back under the rug where they belong.

This is what we see playing out in men's lives: We hide and mask anger. We internalize pressure. We bury losses. We deny being wounded. We withdraw in the face of hard truth. We perceive openness as weakness. We push people away. We change the scenery. We keep secrets. We ignore the facts. We deceive ourselves. We close off. We fear failure. We deflect mistakes. We blame others. We excuse ourselves from feeling the hurts of others. We hide struggles. We change the subject.

These are not the reasons God gave us emotions! He gave them to us because He has emotions, and we are made in His image. He also gave them to us so we could process them with Him and with other men.

Connect with the Word

Read Proverbs 28:13.

1. What is the downside of keeping secrets? Why is it not okay for us to pretend to be okay or all together?

2. What do we find on the other side of confession? How does this compare to what we often think will happen?

Read Ephesians 5:11-14; James 5:16.

3. We know we need to confess our sins to God, but why do you think God tells us to confess our sins to one another as well? (See 1 John 1:9.)

4. According to the passage in Ephesians, what happens when we expose our secrets?

5. Based on these passages, what is the outcome of practicing biblical openness and confession? What does that look like today in practical terms?

Connect with the Group

Group Opener
Read the group opener aloud and discuss the questions that follow.

One time when I [Kenny] was in Sacramento, a guy confronted me about the issue of confession by asking point-blank: "So, Kenny, what's in it for me if I take the risk and confess?"

"Do you want more of God's power in your life?" I responded.

"Yes."

"Do you want to deal Satan a right-hand straight to the jaw?"

"Absolutely," he smiled.

"Do you want people to trust you and be close to you?"

"Sure."

"Do you want God to use you more?"

"With all my heart."

"Good. Then no secrets."

Someone once said, "The greatest weakness is to be conscious of none." I wish I knew the guy's name so I could give him credit for helping me see why God has given us confession as a tool for spiritual growth. The Scriptures encourage honest confession because it produces awesome results in the life of God's man.

When God said to the apostle Paul, "My power is made perfect in weakness" (2 Corinthians 12:9), He was saying that when God's man is at his most vulnerable place, that's when God's power flows most freely toward him. Confession puts us in that place.[3]

Discussion Questions

a. What are the benefits and the drawbacks of confessing to other men in a small group? Why is confession hard for men today?

---

3. Arterburn and Luck, *Every Man, God's Man*, 159-60.

b. What are the practical benefits of being honest about where you are really at or what you are struggling with?

c. How do think the Enemy views confession? Why?

d. What help does confession give to those who hear it in a safe group context?

e. When have you experienced the benefits of confessing a struggle to another brother?

f. How can we help other men feel safe to share their most personal struggles?

Standing Strong

Is there something in your past that you have never told anyone—
something that *needs* to come out? Will you commit to sharing it
with another man you trust? Why or why not?

Is something happening in your life right now that needs to be
shared with another man? If so, what is the issue in a nutshell, and
who do you need to share it with?

empowered to encourage

Key Verse

The LORD is witness between you and me. (1 Samuel 20:42)

Goals for Growth

- Embrace the responsibility of being a source of encouragement to others.
- Learn to allow other men to encourage us spiritually and personally.
- Identify specific ways we can encourage others.

Head Start

Several years ago my friends and I (Kenny) met at the local bagel shop for the purpose of reconnecting with one another as men. We needed to do this because, while we were accustomed to connecting socially (with or without our wives), we needed some pure "guy time" to discuss male issues. Even though we had been getting together off and on for years, this meeting was different—especially for me.

When the conversation paused and then steered my way, I said, "When I come here, I don't have the luxury of walking away without doing real business spiritually. This is my one opportunity to get real with people I trust to help me." Let's just say I had everyone's attention.

"Can we just cut the bull and get real honest about at least one thing we know is bugging us—or one thing God is showing us about ourselves that we need to work on? I think guys—including me—are leaving here sometimes without advice or encouragement on the one thing they really need the most help with. Can we commit to that?"

HELLO!

Men are good at spin. (I know I am.) Smart friends—the discerning ones—ask good questions, draw a man out, and see if they can encourage him in some way or affirm a godly direction in his life. As we'll see, it's like giving a guy a cup of cold water in the desert.

Connect with the Word

Read 1 Samuel 23:13-18.

1. Before Jonathan showed up, who did David have around him?

2. What could Jonathan do for David that six hundred other men could not? Why did David need Jonathan more than his entire army?

3. What specific issues was David dealing with that Jonathan addressed? What did Jonathan specifically do for David that David couldn't do for himself?

4. What did it cost Jonathan to do what he did for David? What did he risk?

5. Why do you think these two men sealed their relationship with a covenant (promise) before the Lord?

6. Why does adding this spiritual dimension to your friendships make them stronger?

Connect with the Group

Group Opener
Read the group opener aloud and discuss the questions that follow.

A number of years ago, when I (Todd) lived in Chicago, I experienced a real job crisis. It happened so fast, I was thoroughly caught off guard. It knocked the air out of me. Facing an uncertain future and living far away from home and the support of family and friends, I struggled to cope with my crisis alone.

My midweek call back home to my brother in California was a tough one. I didn't quite know what to say. Yet I guess I didn't need to say much. Dave and my brother-in-law, Bob, caught a red-eye flight into O'Hare that weekend and arrived Saturday morning.

Their sacrificial act of encouragement was more than I could ever have hoped for. Here were two of my closest buddies, reaching out to me in a mega-act of kindness. And I was hurting more than I realized. The fact that they would spend the money and time away from their families to trek halfway across the country just to encourage me meant more to me than any phone call or card I received during my hardship.

We ended up having a great weekend together. We rented cross-county skis and headed for a forest preserve. That night we took a train into the city for dinner. By Sunday I realized we hadn't even talked much about the career crisis I was facing. We didn't need to. I just needed to know someone cared about me and what I was going through. A show of love well worth its price!

Discussion Questions

a. When have you hit rock bottom in a career crisis or other kind of difficulty? Who helped pull you out of the depths?

b. Would you ever do something like Dave and Bob did? Why or why not?

c. What does spiritual encouragement look like among men? What things often prevent us from encouraging other men spiritually?

d. In 1 Samuel 23:18, David and Jonathan made a solemn covenant before the Lord. What would that look like for us as a group?

e. What man has personally strengthened you to do what God is calling you to do for Him? Explain.

f. What will it cost you personally to be a spiritual encourager to someone else?

Standing Strong

How effective are you as a spiritual encourager? How can you tell?

Who do you know who needs encouragement to persevere in their faith? What can you do to encourage this person?

getting into each other's spaces

Key Verse

Let the godly strike me! It will be a kindness! If they reprove me, it is soothing medicine. Don't let me refuse it. (Psalm 141:5, NLT)

Goals for Growth

- Recognize that God encourages loving confrontation among brothers.
- Commit to opening ourselves up to input from godly friends.
- Seek to develop friendships with men who will tell us what we *need* to hear rather than only what we *want* to hear.

Head Start

No friend of mine (Kenny's) joyfully embraces confrontation. Especially when it involves issues in his "personal airspaces" of life. Those are the areas we love to keep close to the chest, under our own personal control, and posted with large signs on the perimeter declaring, NO TRESPASSING!

Some of our razor-wired areas include our financial habits, our relationships with God, our relationships with our spouses, our parenting approaches, and our moral views. These are sensitive areas because they involve our personal values and core character issues. Very touchy subjects!

I will never forget one night when two guys in the inner circle of my life stopped by to visit. What started out as a friendly meal turned into what felt like a fish fry…and the fish was me! Like skilled surgeons who knew exactly where to go and what to look for, they started making loving cuts in order to help me see the folly of masking over some serious issues arising between my wife and me. To put it mildly, when the conversation turned (on me), and the lights shined into the private corners of my life, it felt like a brutal stabbing rather than a benevolent surgery.

My defenses came up and out, but my friends have spines. They were strong and loving enough to break down my resistance and help me see the truth in their words. Was it uncomfortable? Definitely. Was it necessary? Absolutely.

But it was all done out of deep love. For me.

As we'll see, the test of a true friend is his ability to engage in loving confrontation. In fact, you really don't have a true friendship unless you willing to confront each other when it's needed. Confrontation requires courage and a strong relationship on both sides. And, most important, it requires trust in God and the man He is using—the man called your friend.

Connect with the Word

Read Proverbs 27:5-6; James 5:19-20.

1. What does an open rebuke look like in a healthy relationship? How can a rebuke demonstrate love?

2. How do you wound, but not kill, a friend?

3. To what extent do you need to trust your confronter in order to be helped by him? What kind of friend is able, in your view, to confront in love for good effect? What has to be there?

4. What's the difference between being nice and expressing true care and concern for someone?

5. According to these passages, what kinds of friends do men really need?

6. What picture do you see in James? What does James say is the result of turning a man away from sin and back toward God?

Connect with the Word

Group Opener
Why are we afraid to really get into the "personal airspaces" of one another's lives?

Discussion Questions

a. Why are we so uncomfortable with confrontation? What might help to change our perspective?

b. Why do you think both Solomon and James present this issue as if there is no other option for God's man? What's at stake here?

c. According to James 5:20, when do you know that confronting is the right thing to do?

d. What steps can we take to begin practicing this kind of confrontation in our group? What will it require?

Standing Strong

Are you personally open to healthy confrontation? Why or why not?

Do you know someone who needs to be lovingly confronted? Are you willing to get into his space and express your concern? Why or why not? What steps will you take to confront your friend?

Give someone—a man you respect spiritually and trust personally—
the freedom to speak into your life if they see or sense anything that
might not be consistent with God's plan for you.

stretching one another to greatness for God

Key verse

For this reason I remind you to fan into flame the gift of God, which is in you through the laying on of my hands. (2 Timothy 1:6)

Goals for Growth

- Understand God's true purpose for friendships among His men.
- Recognize the need to help one another discover our personal ministry and mission on earth.
- Commission one another to do the work God is calling us to do for Him.

Head Start

Two years ago I (Kenny) left my job to launch Every Man Ministries. This was a new venture with a lot of unknowns. It was during this season of risk that Todd sent me the following letter:

Dear Kenny,

I often reflect back on the day you came by my office and told me you felt God leading you to help other men. Working with you on this the last four years has brought joy to my days. I have met few men with a passion to live with such tenacity as you. You have an uncontrollable drive to see men made new in Christ and walk free from sin and guilt. You desire to see men live out their manhood in the context of real life.

All men die; few men really live. This could characterize your life. You have chosen a life that will not give you much of the world's goods. For that you will be blessed. As a result, you have become a model, a mentor, and a magnet for men. Attracted by your very life, they strive to be like the Christ who lives in you and through you.

Most men are nice. Few are dangerous. You are dangerous. You are willing to risk it all to see men complete in Christ.

Love you, brother,

Todd

Do you think this letter encouraged me and stretched me to keep pushing myself spiritually—to go for it? King Solomon said it this way, "Like apples of gold in settings of silver is a word spoken in right circumstances." (Proverbs 25:11, NASB).

In our final session we are going to look at the most significant way to help a friend: by stretching him to do something great for God. Sometimes we don't realize how a few well-chosen words can make a good man great.

Connect with the Word

Read 2 Timothy 1:1-8

1. Who's missing from Timothy's family in the passage? What role did Paul play in Timothy's life?

2. What credibility does verse 3 give Paul to say what he says later on in the passage? What message does this send to Timothy?

3. What do you think it means to "fan into flame" the gifts of God within us (verse 6)?

4. What gifts has God already given every man in addition to his talents (verse 7)?

5. How was Paul stretching Timothy (verse 8)? Where was Paul taking Timothy in his faith?

Read Proverbs 16:24; 18:21; 25:11.

6. What do these passages say about the importance of the words we speak into another man's life?

7. How do encouraging and affirming words stretch men to greatness?

Connect with the Group

Group Opener

In what practical ways can we push one another to greater service in advancing God's kingdom?

Discussion Questions

a. How do we help one another overcome our fear of stepping out and serving God?

b. According to 2 Timothy 2:7 and Proverbs 18:21, what is the key that empowers God's man to successfully fulfill his purpose on earth and use his gifts? What's our job? What's God's job?

c. What does it mean to be bold in our faith? What, if anything, is holding you back from encouraging another man to be bold in his faith? How can you verbally affirm another man's faith as Paul affirmed Timothy's?

d. Pick one guy in the group and affirm what you see God doing in his life. In what specific areas would you encourage him to step out more in his service to God? What steps would you encourage him to take to facilitate God's work in his life?

Standing Strong

Based upon what you've learned in this study, what can you do (and say) in the coming months to affirm God's work in the lives of other men? to challenge others to use their gifts to the fullest? to encourage others toward a deeper and bolder expression of their faith?

Pray for one another, asking God to strengthen each man's faith and service to Him.

small-group resources

leader tips

What if men aren't doing the Connect with the Word section before our small-group session?
Don't be discouraged. You set the pace. If you are doing the study and regularly referring to it in conversations with your men throughout the week, they will pick up on its importance. Here are some suggestions to motivate the men in your group to do their home Bible study:

- Send out a midweek e-mail in which you share your answer to one of the study questions. This shows them that you are personally committed to and involved in the study.
- Ask the guys to hit "respond to all" on their e-mail program and share one insight from that week's Bible study with the entire group. Encourage them to send it out before the next small-group session.
- Every time you meet, ask each man in the group to share one insight from his home study.

What if men are not showing up for small group?
This might mean they are losing a sin battle and don't want to admit it to the group. Or they might be consumed with other priorities. Or maybe they don't think they're getting anything out of the group. Here are some suggestions for getting the guys back each week:

- Affirm them when they show up, and tell them how much it means to you that they make small group a priority.

- From time to time, ask them to share one reason they think small group is important to them.
- Regularly call or send out an e-mail the day before you meet to remind them you're looking forward to seeing them.
- Check in with any guy who has missed more than one session, and find out what's going on in his life.
- Get some feedback from the men. You may need to adjust your style. Listen and learn.

What if group discussion is not happening?

You are a discussion facilitator. You have to keep guys involved in the discussion or you'll lose them. You can engage a man who isn't sharing by saying, "Chuck, you've been quiet. What do you think about this question or discussion?" You should also be prepared to share your own personal stories that are related to the discussion questions. You'll set the example by the kind of sharing you do.

What if one man is dominating the group time?

You have to deal with it. If you don't, men will stop showing up. No one wants to hear from just one guy all the time. It will quickly kill morale. Meet with the guy in person and privately. Firmly but gently suggest that he allow others more time to talk. Be positive and encouraging, but truthful. You might say, "Bob, I notice how enthusiastic you are about the group and how you're always prepared to share your thoughts with the group. But there are some pretty quiet guys in the group too. Have you noticed? Would you be willing to help me get them involved in speaking up?"

How do I get the guys in my group more involved?

Give them something to do. Ask one guy to bring a snack. Invite another to lead the prayer time (ask in advance). Have one guy sub for you one week as the leader. (Meet with him beforehand to walk through the group program and the time allotments for each segment.) Encourage another guy to lead a subgroup.

What if guys are not being vulnerable during the Standing Strong or prayer times?

You model openness. You set the pace. Honesty breeds honesty. Vulnerability breeds vulnerability. Are you being vulnerable and honest about your own problems and struggles? (This doesn't mean that you have to spill your guts each week or reveal every secret of your life.) Remember, men want an honest, on-their-level leader who strives to walk with God. (Also, as the leader, you need an accountability partner, perhaps another group leader.)

What will we do at the first session?

We encourage you to open by discussing the **Small-Group Covenant** we've included in this resource section. Ask the men to commit to the study, and then discuss how long it will take your group to complete each session. (We suggest 75-90 minute sessions.) Men find it harder to come up with excuses for missing a group session if they have made a covenant to the other men right at the start.

Begin to identify ways certain men can play a more active role in small group. Give away responsibility. You won't feel as burdened, and your men will grow from the experience. Keep in mind that this process can take a few weeks. Challenge men to fulfill one of the group roles identified later in this resource section. If no one steps forward to fill a role, say to one of the men, "George, I've noticed that you are comfortable praying in a group. Would you lead us each week during that time?"

How can we keep the group connected after we finish a study?
Begin talking about starting another Bible study before you finish this eight-week study. (There are six studies to choose from in the Every Man Bible study series.) Consider having a social time at the conclusion of the study, and encourage the men to invite a friend. This will help create momentum and encourage growth as you launch into another study with your group. There are probably many men in your church or neighborhood who aren't in small groups but would like to be. Be the kind of group that includes others.

As your group grows, consider choosing an apprentice leader who can take half the group into another room for the **Connect with the Group** time. That subgroup can stay together for prayer, or you can reconvene as a large group during that time. You could also meet for discussion as a large group, and then break into subgroups for **Standing Strong** and **prayer.**

If your group doubles in size, it might be a perfect opportunity to release your apprentice leader with half the group to start another group. Allow men to pray about this and make a decision as a group. Typically, the relational complexities that come into play when a small group births a new group work themselves out. Allow guys to choose which group they'd like to be a part of. If guys are slow in choosing one group or another, ask them individually to select one of the groups. Take the lead in making this happen.

Look for opportunities for your group to serve in the church or community. Consider a local outreach project or a short-term missions trip. There are literally hundreds of practical ways you can serve the Lord in outreach. Check with your church leaders to learn the needs in your congregation or community. Create some interest by sending out scouts who will return with a report for the group. Serving keeps men from becoming self-focused and ingrown. When you serve as a group, you will grow as a group.

using this study in a large-group format

Many church leaders are looking for biblically based curriculum that can be used in a large-group setting, such as a Sunday-school class, or for small groups within an existing larger men's group. Each of the Every Man Bible studies can be adapted for this purpose. In addition, this curriculum can become a catalyst for churches wishing to launch men's small groups or to build a men's ministry in their church.

Getting Started

Begin by getting the word out to men in your church, inviting them to join you for a men's study based on one of the topics in the Every Man Bible study series. You can place a notice in your church bulletin, have the pastor announce it from the pulpit, or pursue some other means of attracting interest.

Orientation Week

Arrange your room with round tables and chairs. Put approximately six chairs at each table.

Start your class in prayer and introduce your topic with a short but motivational message from any of the scriptures used in the Bible study. Hand out the curriculum and challenge the men to do their homework before each class. During this first session give the men some discussion questions based upon an overview of the material and have them talk things through just within their small group around the table.

Just before you wrap things up, have each group select a table host or leader. You can do this by having everyone point at once to the person at their table they feel would best facilitate discussion for future meetings.

Ask those newly elected table leaders to stay after for a few minutes, and offer them an opportunity to be further trained as small-group leaders as they lead discussions throughout the course of the study.

Subsequent Weeks

Begin in prayer. Then give a short message (15-25 minutes) based upon the scripture used for that lesson. Pull out the most motivating topics or points and strive to make the discussion relevant to the life of an everyday man and his world. Then leave time for each table to work through the discussion questions listed in the curriculum. Be sure the discussion facilitators at each table close in prayer.

At the end of the eight sessions, you might want to challenge each "table group" to become a small group, inviting them to meet regularly with their new small-group leader and continue building the relationships they've begun.

prayer request record

Date:
Name:
Prayer Request:
Praise:

Date:
Name:
Prayer Request:
Praise:

Date:
Name:
Prayer Request:
Praise:

Date:
Name:
Prayer Request:
Praise:

Date:
Name:
Prayer Request:
Praise:

defining group roles

Group Leader: Leads the lesson and facilitates group discussion.

Apprentice Leader: Assists the leader as needed, which may include leading the lesson.

Refreshment Coordinator: Maintains a list of who will provide refreshments. Calls group members on the list to remind them to bring what they signed up for.

Prayer Warrior: Serves as the contact person for prayer between sessions. Establishes a list of those willing to pray for needs that arise. Maintains the prayer-chain list and activates the chain as needed by calling the first person on the list.

Social Chairman: Plans any desired social events during group sessions or at another scheduled time. Gathers members for planning committees as needed.

small-group roster

Name:
Address:
Phone: E-mail:

Name:
Address:
Phone: E-mail:

Name:
Address:
Phone: E-mail:

Name:
Address:
Phone: E-mail:

Name:
Address:
Phone: E-mail:

Name:
Address:
Phone: E-mail:

spiritual checkup

Your answers to the statements below will help you determine which areas you need to work on in order to grow spiritually. Mark the appropriate letter to the left of each statement. Then make a plan to take one step toward further growth in each area. Don't forget to pray for the Lord's wisdom before you begin. Be honest. Don't be overly critical or rationalize your weaknesses.

Y = Yes
S = Somewhat or Sometimes
N = No

My Spiritual Connection with Other Believers

____I am developing relationships with Christian friends.

____I have joined a small group.

____I am dealing with conflict in a biblical manner.

____I have become more loving and forgiving than I was a year ago.

____I am a loving and devoted husband and father.

My Spiritual Growth

____I have committed to daily Bible reading and prayer.

____I am journaling on a regular basis, recording my spiritual growth.

____I am growing spiritually by studying the Bible with others.

____I am honoring God in my finances and personal giving.

____I am filled with joy and gratitude for my life, even during trials.

____I respond to challenges with peace and faith instead of anxiety and anger.

____I avoid addictive behaviors (excessive drinking, overeating, watching too much TV, etc.).

Serving Christ and Others

____I am in the process of discovering my spiritual gifts and talents.

____I am involved in ministry in my church.

____I have taken on a role or responsibility in my small group.

____I am committed to helping someone else grow in his spiritual walk.

Sharing Christ with Others

____I care about and am praying for those around me who are unbelievers.

____I share my experience of coming to know Christ with others.

____I invite others to join me in this group or for weekend worship services.

____I am seeing others come to Christ and am praying for this to happen.

____I do what I can to show kindness to people who don't know Christ.

Surrendering My Life for Growth

___I attend church services weekly.

___I pray for others to know Christ, and I seek to fulfill the Great Commission.

___I regularly worship God through prayer, praise, and music, both at church and at home.

___I care for my body through exercise, nutrition, and rest.

___I am concerned about using my energy to serve God's purposes instead of my own.

My Identity in the Lord

___I see myself as a beloved son of God, one whom God loves regardless of my sin.

___I can come to God in all of my humanity and know that He accepts me completely. When I fail, I willingly run to God for forgiveness.

___I experience Jesus as an encouraging Friend and Lord each moment of the day.

___I have an abiding sense that God is on my side. I am aware of His gracious presence with me throughout the day.

___During moments of beauty, grace, and human connection, I lift up praise and thanks to God.

___I believe that using my talents to their fullest pleases the Lord.

___I experience God's love for me in powerful ways.

small-group covenant

As a committed group member, I agree to the following:*

- **Regular Attendance.** I will attend group sessions on time and let everyone know in advance if I can't make it.
- **Group Safety.** I will help create a safe, encouraging environment where men can share their thoughts and feelings without fear of embarrassment or rejection. I will not judge another guy or attempt to fix his problems.
- **Confidentiality.** I will always keep to myself everything that is shared in the group.
- **Acceptance.** I will respect different opinions or beliefs and let Scripture be the teacher.
- **Accountability.** I will make myself accountable to the other group members for the personal goals I share.
- **Friendliness.** I will look for those around me who might join the group and explore their faith with other men.
- **Ownership.** I will prayerfully consider taking on a specific role within the group as the opportunity arises.
- **Spiritual Growth.** I will commit to establishing a daily quiet time with God, which includes doing the homework for this study. I will share with the group the progress I make and the struggles I experience as I seek to grow spiritually.

Signed: _____ Date: _____

---

*   *Permission is given to photocopy and distribute this form to each man in your group. Review this covenant quarterly or as needed.*

about the authors

STEPHEN ARTERBURN is coauthor of the best-selling Every Man series. He is also founder and chairman of New Life Clinics, host of the daily *New Life Live!* national radio program, and creator of the Women of Faith conferences. A nationally known speaker and licensed minister, Stephen has authored more than forty books. He lives with his family in Laguna Beach, California.

KENNY LUCK is president and founder of Every Man Ministries and coauthor of *Every Man, God's Man* and its companion workbook. He is division leader for men's small groups and teaches a men's interactive Bible study at Saddleback Church in Lake Forest, California. He and his wife, Chrissy, have three children and reside in Rancho Santa Margarita, California.

TODD WENDORFF is a graduate of U.C. Berkeley and holds a Th.M. from Talbot School of Theology. He serves as a pastor of men's ministries at Saddleback Church and is an adjunct professor at Biola University. He is an author of the Doing Life Together Bible study series. Todd and his wife, Denise, live with their three children in Trabuco Canyon, California.

every man's battle
workshops
from New Life Ministries

new Life Ministries receives hundreds of calls every month from Christian men who are struggling to stay pure in the midst of daily challenges to their sexual integrity and from pastors who are looking for guidance in how to keep fragile marriages from falling apart all around them.

As part of our commitment to equip individuals to win these battles, New Life Ministries has developed biblically based workshops directly geared to answer these needs. These workshops are held several times per year around the country.

- Our workshops for men are structured to equip men with the tools necessary to maintain sexual integrity and enjoy healthy, productive relationships.

- Our workshops for church leaders are targeted to help pastors and men's ministry leaders develop programs to help families being attacked by this destructive addiction.

Some comments from previous workshop attendees:

"An awesome, life-changing experience. Awesome teaching, teacher, content and program." —DAVE

"God has truly worked a great work in me since the EMB workshop. I am fully confident that with God's help, I will be restored in my ministry position. Thank you for your concern. I realize that this is a battle, but I now have the weapons of warfare as mentioned in Ephesians 6:10, and I am using them to gain victory!" —KEN

"It's great to have a workshop you can confidently recommend to anyone without hesitation, knowing that it is truly life changing. Your labors are not in vain!" —DR. BRAD STENBERG, Pasadena, CA

If sexual temptation is threatening your marriage or your church, please call **1-800-NEW-LIFE** to speak with one of our specialists.

every man conferences
revolutionizing local churches

"This is a revolutionary conference that has the potential to change the world. Thanks Kenny! The fire is kindled!" —B.J.

"The conference was tremendous and exactly what I needed personally. The church I pastor is starting a men's group to study the material launched at this conference. This is truly an answer to my prayer!" —DAVID

"Thank you! Thank you! Thank you! I didn't know how much I needed this. I look forward to working through the material with my small group." —BOB

"It's the only conference I have attended where I will go back and read my notes!" —ROGER

"This is a conference every man should attend." —KARL

"After years of waffling with God, I am ready to welcome Him into my every day life. Thanks for giving me the tools to help me develop a relationship with God." —GEORGE

"This revolutionary conference is the next wave of men's ministry in America." —STEVE ARTERBURN, Coauthor of *Every Man's Battle*

If you want to :
- address the highest felt need issues among men
- launch or grow your men's ministry
- connect your men in small groups around God's Word
- and reach seeking men with the Gospel

Join with other churches or sponsor an every man conference in your area.

For information on booking Kenny Luck or scheduling an Every Man Conference contact Every Man Ministries at 949-766-7830 or email at everymanministries@aol.com. For more information on Every Man events, visit our website at everymanministries.com.

start a bible study
and connect with others
who want to be God's man.

If you enjoyed the *Every Man, God's Man Workbook,* you'll love the Every Man Bible Studies, designed to help you discover, own, and build on convictions grounded in God's word.